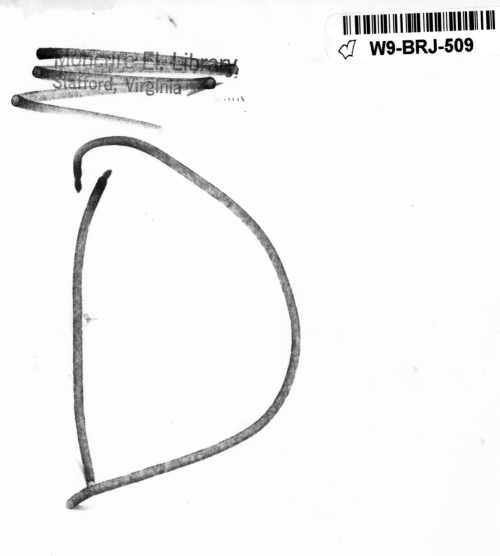

DECOUPAGE CRAFTS

BY FLORENCE TEMKO
Illustrated by Linda Winchester

DOUBLEDAY & COMPANY, INC., GARDEN CITY, NEW YORK

1

To Ronald for being Ronald

Thanks to my husband; Henry Petzal, for his continuing encouragement and to Madeline Anish, Donald Davis and Neisa DeWitt, for their help, each in a special way.

Other books by Florence Temko

PAPER CUTTING

FELT CRAFT

SELF-STICK CRAFT

PAPERFOLDING TO BEGIN WITH

PAPER: FOLDED, CUT, SCULPTED

IN PREPARATION: MAKE SOMETHING!

745.54
Tem

Library of Congress Cataloging in Publication Data

Temko, Florence
    Decoupage crafts

11370

    SUMMARY: Introduces the beginner to the art of decoupage and gives instructions for a variety of projects.
1. Decoupage—Juvenile literature. [1. Decoupage. 2. Handicraft] I. Winchester, Linda. II. Title.
TT870.T444   745.54
ISBN 0-385-01503-8 Trade
      0-385-07791-2 Prebound
Library of Congress Catalog Card Number 74–33666

2

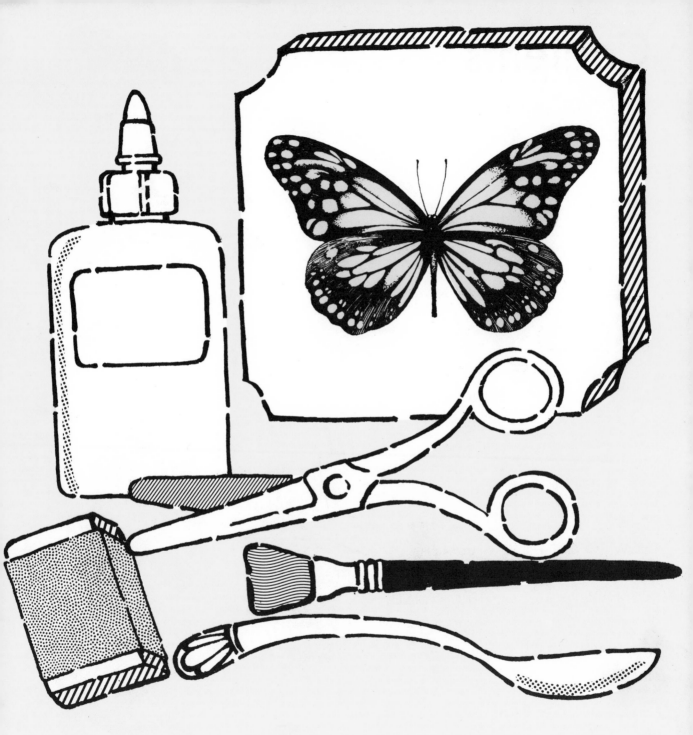

Contents

Contents

A Page for Adults

This book is an introduction to decoupage for beginners of all ages, although the illustrations are designed to appeal to children and teen-agers. This craft is well within their ability and the basic steps are great fun: children like to sand a board, cut out pictures and arrange them, wipe on layers of glue and finally glaze the decoupages with many coats of varnish.

The book begins with a picture made by bonding a print to a wooden board. This project involves a minimum number of steps. The next project adds the step of cutting a print. Further steps are added one by one, until the reader has a pretty good idea what decoupage is all about. Once the basics are mastered, there is no limit to the many things that can be made. As you leaf through the book you will see that not only pictures, but toys, jewelry, furniture, knick-knacks and other things lend themselves to decoupaging. Many suggestions are made to send the child's imagination on flights of fancy. The illustrations reflect everyday hobbies, travel, sports activities and other current preoccupations, as well as the more traditional designs.

The age-old craft of decoupage has recently been revived, due to the invention of new plastic finishes which make it easy to achieve beautiful results quickly. To help you and your youngster choose among the bewildering profusion of brand names, I have provided a listing at the end of the book, which describes the properties of various materials. I have selected them for ease of handling and safety for children. At the time of writing, they have the widest geographical distribution.

My aim in writing this book is to provide information about the craft of decoupage and invite experimentation and discovery. Readers learn not only a new craft, but develop their manual dexterity and design ability. At the first try, in selecting and arranging cut-outs, their innate creative ability is encouraged to express itself.

About Decoupage

Decoupage sounds a bit mysterious and everybody seems to have a different idea what it is. The word is pronounced day-koo-paj (rhymes with garage), and comes from the French word *coupage*, meaning cutting. Generally decoupage is the craft of gluing a paper cut-out to a wooden board and varnishing it many times until the coats of varnish are as high as the paper. The picture and varnish blend into each other. It looks as though the picture is painted on the board and even when you run your finger over the top you cannot tell where the print ends. In this way, anyone can decorate with printed designs on wood, glass, metal or cardboard.

It is a lot of fun to sandpaper the board, make paper cut-outs, paste them on the board and brush on many layers of varnish. With the help of this book, you can find out exactly how to make pictures, toys, greeting cards, trophies and many other things. Have you received a special birthday card? Now you can preserve it with a clear permanent finish. Collect magazine illustrations of football players and combine them in a collage. Try decorating a treasure box with flowers cut from stationery. You can use maps, newspaper cartoons, baseball cards and pictures of your favorite hobby or sport. If you are a stamp collector, decoupage some duplicates on an album cover. You can preserve your favorite crayoned or painted pictures. As you look through the book, you will come up with a thousand different ideas for using decoupage. When your project is completed, you'll be proud to say: "I made it!" Keep the things for yourself, give them away as birthday gifts or you can even sell them. They could help you raise money for scouting, a youth group or a hospital.

And now have fun with decoupage!

Read This First

* FOLLOW ALL THE WRITTEN DIRECTIONS AND LOOK AT THE PICTURES. TOGETHER THEY MAKE IT EASY FOR YOU.

* FOLLOW CHAPTER 1 STEP BY STEP. THEN YOU ARE READY TO TRY ANY OF THE PROJECTS IN THE OTHER CHAPTERS.

* WHEN A STEP IS DESCRIBED FOR THE FIRST TIME, THE HEADING IS SET IN A BOX LIKE THIS: SANDING. IN THIS WAY YOU KNOW YOU ARE LEARNING SOMETHING NEW.

* ALWAYS WORK ON NEWSPAPER, SO THAT THE GLUES AND VAR-NISHES DO NOT GET ON FURNITURE.

* *MEASUREMENTS:* All sizes are given in inches and are then followed by parentheses. The numbers in the parentheses repeat the measurements, but in metric system centimeters. In order to avoid fractions, these measurements may not always be exactly the same.

1

Basic Steps

This chapter shows how to decoupage three pictures and a box in the simplest ways. It is the most important part of the book.

A Picture with a Magazine Illustration

You need:

A wooden board
A picture cut from a magazine
Fine sandpaper wrapped around a wooden block
Podge, with a brush or small piece of sponge
   (If you do not have Podge, see page 19 for what you can use
   instead.)
A spoon or rubber roller

SANDING

1 Sand board with sandpaper in the direction of the grain of the wood (**with** the lines in the wood), until it is very smooth. Run tip of your finger over the wood and sand until it feels even.

SEALING

2 Brush or wipe on Podge with a brush or small piece of sponge. Let it dry for at least 10 minutes until the Podge looks clear and not white any more.

3 Cut a magazine illustration to fit on the wooden board.

PASTING

4 When your first coat of Podge is dry, brush or wipe on another coat. Put magazine illustration on at once. Rub picture with the back of the spoon for a few minutes to move out any air bubbles. Let dry for 10 minutes.

GLAZING

5 Brush or wipe on three more coats of Podge, waiting at least 10 minutes between each coat.

A Picture with a Cut-out

You need:

A wooden board
A greeting card with a bold print
Podge, with a brush or small piece of sponge
Fine sandpaper
A spoon or roller
Picture hanger

SANDING

1 Sand the board with sandpaper in the direction of the grain of the wood, until it is very smooth.

SEALING

2 Wipe or brush on Podge. Let it dry for 10 minutes.

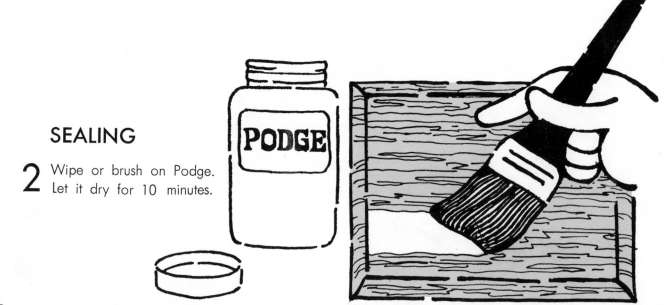

CUTTING

3 Cut out the design from a greeting card.

PASTING

4 When first coat of Podge has dried, wipe on another coat and place cut-out on it. Rub picture for a few minutes to move out any air bubbles. Let dry.

GLAZING

5 Brush or wipe on three more coats of Podge, waiting at least 10 minutes between coats.

FINISHING

6 Attach picture hanger to the back of the board.

13

A Crayoned Picture

You need:

A wooden board
A piece of drawing paper a little smaller than the board
Crayons
Clear varnish (brush-on or spray type)
A grocery carton
Sandpaper wrapped around a wooden block
Podge, with a brush or small piece of sponge
Spoon or roller
Picture hanger

CRAYONING A PICTURE

1 Crayon a picture on the drawing paper. (Make several pictures and decoupage the one you like best.)

SEALING THE PAPER

2 Varnish the picture on one side. Let it dry and varnish the other side. IF YOU USE SPRAY VARNISH, PUT THE PICTURE INSIDE A GROCERY BOX TO PROTECT THE FURNITURE IN THE ROOM.

3 Sand board with sandpaper in the direction of the grain until it is very smooth.

4 Seal the wooden board by brushing or wiping on Podge. Let it dry for at least 10 minutes.

5 When your first coat of Podge is dry, brush or wipe on another coat. Place crayoned picture on at once.

6 Rub picture for a few minutes to move out any air bubbles. Let dry for at least 10 minutes.

7 Brush or wipe on three more coats of Podge, waiting at least 10 minutes between each coat.

8 Attach picture hanger to the back of the board.

A Box

You need:

A wooden box with a cover, or
A deep cardboard gift box
4 or more baseball cards
Fine sandpaper wrapped around a wooden block
Podge, with a brush or small piece of sponge
A spoon or roller

CHOOSING BOX DECORATIONS

1 Choose a baseball card for the cover. Use the other baseball cards to cut out mitts, bats and caps for decorating the sides.

2 First decoupage the top of the lid, by sanding, sealing, pasting and glazing as shown in chapter 1. Follow each step carefully.

3 Decoupage TWO SIDES of the box, with the small cut-outs arranged in a nice way. Then decoupage the other two sides.

4 When the lid is dry, brush several coats of Podge on the edges of the lid.

2

Basic Materials

This chapter lists materials needed for making decoupages and is divided into sections. For every decoupage choose ONE thing from each section.

Object

Choose one:

Wooden board, also called
   a plaque
Wooden box
Book ends
Step stool
Other furniture
Frame
Wastepaper basket
Empty bottle
Wood or metal tray
Cardboard
Poster board

Notebook binder
Photo album
Scrapbook cover
Papier-mâché objects
Ceramic figures
Football helmets
Sneakers
Rocks
Bowls
Styrofoam forms
File boxes

Decorations

Choose one:

Magazine illustration
Giftwrap paper
Decoupage print
A cut-out you make yourself
Postcard
Coloring book page
Catalogue illustration
Crayons
Felt tip pens
Acrylic paints

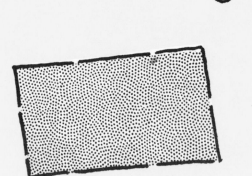

Sandpaper
to smooth wood

Choose only if object is made of wood. The best kind to use is numbered 000 or called garnet.

Scissors

A pair with long blades, **AND**
A pair with short blades, about 4" (10 cm) long,
A pair of cuticle scissors (if you like)

Applicator
for using with sealers, varnishes, glue and paint

Brush, about 1" (3 cm) wide
Small pieces of sponge, about 1" (3.cm) square

Glazes
for sealing wood or paper, for glazing and varnishing

Podge, called Mod-Podge, Fun Podge and Twinkle Podge. Clear acrylic spray, called Craft Spray,
Krylon. or other brand names. When you use spray, place the object inside a grocery carton,
to protect the furniture and floor. Clear wood finish, Deft or other brand; any home varnish,
except spar varnish. Follow directions on the labels.

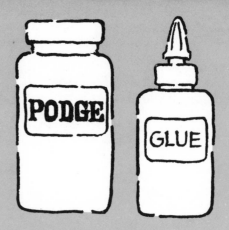

Glue
for pasting down prints

White glue, Sobo or Elmer's
Podge (Mod-Podge, Fun Podge or Twinkle Podge)

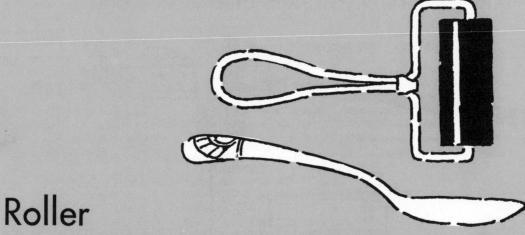

Roller
for pressing down paper

A spoon
A rubber roller called a brayer
A wallpaper roller

For every decoupage you need a number of different materials. In the rest of the book you will sometimes find the words "Basic Decoupage Materials" at the beginning of instructions. This means you will need things from the lists in this chapter. Additional materials will be listed for each decoupage.

3

How to Cut Prints and Make Paper Cut-outs

This chapter shows how to cut paper; how to arrange parts of prints into your own designs; how to make different kinds of cut-outs from colored paper, and many other ideas.

How to Cut

There are a few tricks to cutting paper which you should know:

SCISSORS

To cut paper for decoupaging, you should have two pairs of scissors; one pair with fairly long blades for cutting outlines, and another pair about 4" (10 cm) long with pointed blades for fine work. These are sometimes called decoupage scissors. Cuticle scissors with small curved blades are also good to have.

TO CUT CURVES

The **hand holding the scissors is kept still** and the other **hand, holding the paper, moves.**

FINE CUTTING

Cut the main outline first. Then cut the fine lines. The illustration shows the two steps: the colored line is cut first; then the black line.

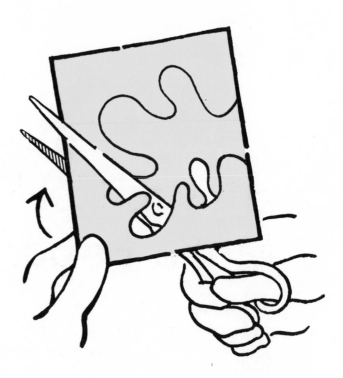

Cutting Prints

Any printed picture or words can be used for decoupaging. Prints made specially for decoupage are sold in arts and crafts shops, and some other stores. These prints are made from strong paper, just right for this work. You can also use illustrations from magazines, advertisements, catalogues, postcards, greeting cards, wallpaper or labels.

You can use the whole illustration or cut separate parts and arrange them in your own way. Some decoupage prints are made for cutting apart. They may be a collection of flowers or leaves, or a pattern for a border design.

This shows a plaque made with a complete print.

This shows a plaque made with the same print cut into parts.

Cut-outs from Colored Paper

You can cut your own pictures from white or colored papers. Decoupage these cut-outs in the same way as a print.

CUT-OUTS FROM FLAT PAPER

You need:

A wooden board
Paper in red, blue and yellow or other colors
Pencil, scissors
Podge, with a brush or piece of sponge
Fine sandpaper wrapped around a wooden block
White glue
A spoon or roller

1 Brush or wipe Podge on board and let dry.

2 Cut paper into shapes.

3 Arrange them in a design you like. This picture shows a future city.

4 Glue design on the board; press down design with back of spoon or roller. Continue with decoupaging steps you learned in chapter 1.

CUT-OUTS FROM FOLDED PAPER

You can fold paper before you cut out a design. In this way, the pattern is multiplied and you get all sorts of surprises.

You need:

A piece of colored paper
Pencil, scissors
Basic decoupage materials (see chapter 2)

1 Fold paper in half.

2 Draw **half** the outline of a heart against the **folded** edge.

3 Cut out through both layers of paper. Unfold.

4 Use the cut-out as a decoupage decoration.

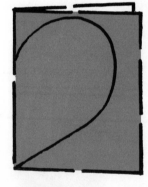

More Designs

CUT-OUTS FROM PAPER FOLDED IN QUARTERS

You need:

Thin colored paper the same size as the board you want to decoupage
Pencil
Basic decoupage materials (see chapter 2)

1 Fold paper in quarters.

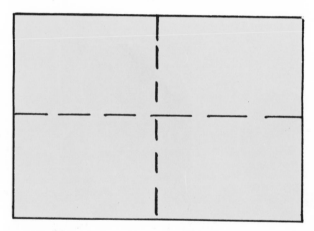

2 Draw small designs starting from the four edges of the paper as shown. Do not draw a line all the way across from one edge to the other.

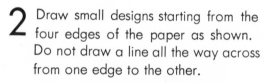

3 Cut on the lines you have drawn. Unfold paper.

4 Make several cut-outs and decoupage the one you like best.

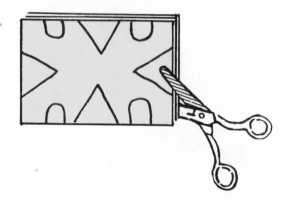

More Folded Paper Designs

Fold paper in pleats or wedges and then cut small pieces away on the edges. Unfold and decoupage.

Experiment with other ways of folding the paper before cutting it. You can cut the folded paper without first drawing the design in pencil.

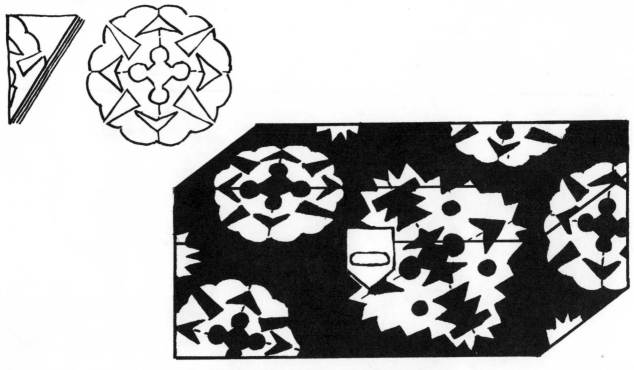

Box with Snowflakes

Picture Cut-outs

Picture cut-outs are usually made from paper which is black on one side and white on the other, but you can use paper in any dark shade.

You need:

Dark paper
Pencil
Basic decoupage materials (see chapter 2)

1 Draw picture on white side of paper.
Draw bold shapes which are easy to cut out.

2 Cut out the picture.

3 Decoupage picture on the board.

INSIDE CUTTING

To make your picture cut-out more interesting, you may want to cut out a small piece of paper from inside a large area. Good examples are eyes, nose and mouth in a face. Pierce the paper with the point of your small pair of scissors and cut around the pierced hole.

This paper cut-out comes from China and shows very fine inside cutting.

Pasting Cut-outs

You need:

A paper cut-out
White glue
A jar lid or small saucer
Basic decoupage materials (see chapter 2)

Seal object and sand if necessary.

Pour a small amount of glue into the jar lid or saucer. Place cut-out on the object exactly where you want it. With your forefinger slide a little glue under one corner; then press it down. Slide glue to the part next to the corner you have already pasted down. Repeat this until the whole picture is done. Gently press down all over with your fingers.

Glaze the picture with several coats of varnish.

Draw an eagle and cut it out. Small extra cut-outs have been added in this Indian decoration.

Napkin Tear-outs

Paper napkins can be used for decoupage and are even easier to use than regular paper. Try napkin tear-outs on Styrofoam eggs and add some glitter.

You need:

Paper napkin with a bold design
Acrylic paint the same color as the background of the napkin
   (With white napkins, gesso is better than paint)
Sobo glue, or other white glue
Basic decoupage supplies

1   Seal object you have chosen.

2   Paint it with acrylic paint or gesso.

3   While paint is drying, tear out the pattern from the paper napkin. With left hand hold pattern and with right hand tear around it. (If you are left-handed, reverse this.)

4   When paint is dry, cover the object with a thin coat of glue. Press torn napkin design in place.

5   Rub gently for about five minutes.

6   Glaze with several coats.

4

Transfers

This chapter shows how to make transfers. Any printed picture is covered with several coats of transfer liquid, which forms a film. Then the paper is rubbed away leaving just the picture on the film. It's magic!

A Transfer on a Canvas Board

You need:

A canvas board (or a piece of cardboard or a plaque)
A print the same size as the board or smaller
A bottle of transfer liquid, called decal-it or Trans-A-Print
A 1" (3 cm) brush
Masking tape
A spoon or a roller
A sponge or paper towels

1 Tape the print on a heavy piece of paper with the masking tape.

2 Shake the bottle of transfer liquid. Put thick heavy lines of liquid near the four edges of the print and then spread the liquid evenly all over the print with the brush. Let dry 15 minutes. Wash out brush with sudsy water.

3 Brush on 5 more coats of liquid and let each coat dry 15 minutes. Wash out the brush each time.

4 Let transfer dry overnight.

5 The next day, take off the masking tape and soak the transfer in warm water in a sink or a pan. After about 2 hours test if the paper peels off. If not, soak longer.

6 When paper is soft enough to peel off, put the picture face down on Formica or other hard surface. Carefully pull the paper away from the film. Rub off the rest of the paper with a wet sponge or paper towels. The transfer is now completed. Let it dry.

7 Glue transfer to the canvas board with transfer liquid. Press it down with the back of a spoon or a roller. Let it dry.

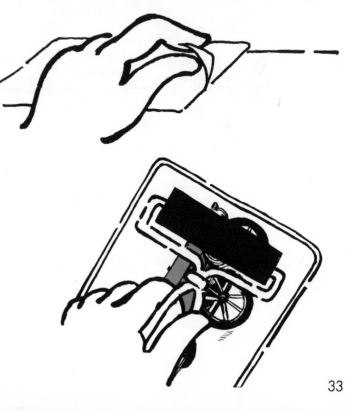

8 Cover the board with the transfer picture with one more coat of the transfer liquid. Let dry.

More Projects

All the projects on the following pages can be decoupaged in the ways already described.

Small Objects

You can decoupage key chains, pendants, and Christmas ornaments quickly. Make several at a time and give as gifts or sell them.

Bull's-eye key chain is made from corrugated cardboard. Both sides of the cardboard are decoupaged with Podge. Chain is bought at a store.

Pendant is also made from cardboard, which is first cut into a triangle.

Christmas ornaments are cut from Styrofoam meat trays, sealed with gesso bought at an art store, and decorated with acrylic paint.

A Wooden Purse

Wooden purses are for sale at arts and crafts stores. Straight sides are easier to decoupage. You can use complete prints, cut-outs or transfers. On curved sides use only small decorations. Full-size prints pucker on the curves and will not look neat.

Toys

You can draw the outline of any kind of animal, cut it from wood or cardboard and then decoupage it. Old scratched toys can be done over too.

A Frame

Wide frames are fun to decoupage and are very good for mirrors.

You need:

A wooden frame at least 1″ (3 cm) wide
Giftwrap paper with small flowers
Acrylic paint
Mirror glass to fit the frame
Brown wrapping paper
Basic decoupage materials (see chapter 2)

1 Paint frame.

2 Cut out flowers from the gift-wrap paper and arrange them on the frame.

3 Decoupage the frame as shown in chapter 1.

4 After decoupaging, fit the mirror glass into the frame. Glue heavy brown wrapping paper to the back, covering the mirror and the frame. Trim brown paper edges.

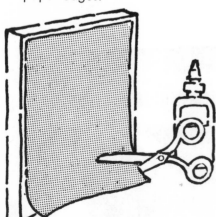

A Name Box

The cut-out design on this box looks like a tree, but if you look closely you can see that it is really a name with a mirror image.

You need:

A box
Paint, acrylic or latex
Colored paper the same size as the lid
Pencil
Wide felt tip pen
Scissors
Basic decoupage materials (see chapter 2)

Folded edge is here

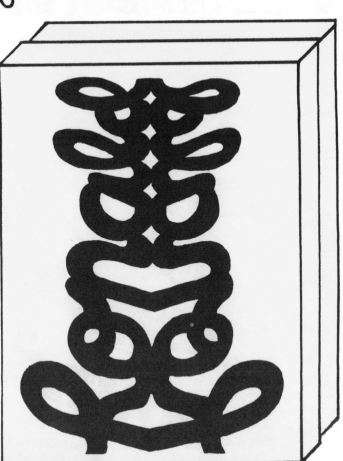

1 Paint the box.

2 Fold the paper in half in the longest direction. If paper is colored on one side and white on the other, color should now be hidden inside. This way, your pencil lines will not show when the box is finished.

3 Draw a diagonal line on the paper. The line does not go all the way into the córner on the right side.

4 Lightly pencil name into the space next to the folded edge. Fill up the whole space, beginning with a large letter. Change writing until it fits well.

5 With wide felt tip pen write over the penciled name.

6 Cut away all parts that are not covered by the writing. Be sure not to cut through the bottom edges of the letters as this would make the paper fall apart. Unfold paper.

7 Decoupage the trick name to the box.

Book Ends

The wood grain in these book ends is used to make the eyes.

Coasters

A set of six coasters is decorated with candy wrappers.

Furniture

This step stool was first painted with regular latex paint. Then the cut print was glued on with Sobo. Finally three coats of clear varnish were wiped on.

After you have decoupaged some of the smaller things shown in the book, you can decoupage furniture, such as chairs, side tables and dressers.

Rock Singer

This funny figure is made from decoupaged rocks. You can also make other people or animals. Collect rocks whenever you see them, on a trip to the country, on the beach or on an empty lot. Gather different sizes and colors of pebbles, stones and rocks. Smooth rocks are easier to decoupage, but any rough spots may be painted to look like eyes or fingers, or whatever you see in the stone.

You need:
2 large stones
2 small stones
Detergent
Paper towels
Podge or clear varnish
Gesso
Acrylic paint
White glue
A cotton ball

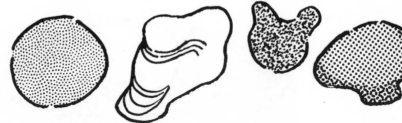

WASHING

1 Wash and scrub stones with detergent. Rinse them well in clear water. Let them dry thoroughly.

2 Seal the stones all over with Podge or a craft spray sealer.

LEVELING (IF NECESSARY)

3 Rough stones may need leveling out. Brush the stones with gesso. Build up several layers of gesso until the stone is smooth.

4 Paint the rocks with acrylic paint. First paint the rocks all over in one color. Then paint on the face, clothing and other decorations.

5 Cover rocks with several coats of Podge or clear varnish.

GLUING ROCKS TOGETHER

6 Glue the rocks together with white glue. If round rocks do not stay glued together, soak a piece of a cotton ball in the glue and wedge it between the two stones. Hold them in place until the glue hardens.

Three-dimensional Decoupage

This chapter shows different ways to make three dimensional decoupages; knobby decoupage, paper tole, foil craft and self-stick decoupage.

Knobby Decoupage

To give depth to a picture you can make some parts of it higher. A good example is a nose, which sticks out of a face, or the balloon shown in the illustration. The instructions show how you can push crushed paper mixed with glue behind the picture, or you can use small lumps of clay or cotton instead.

You need:
A picture
A piece of newspaper about the size of this page
White glue
Toothpicks
Basic decoupage materials (see chapter 2)

1 Seal the wood and seal the picture. Let them dry.

2 Meanwhile, with scissors, cut the newspaper into tiny pieces. Mix them with some white glue and a few drops of water.

3 With a toothpick put a small blob of this mixture on the **back** of the picture where you want it to be higher. Crosses show where to put it.

4 Glue picture to the board and continue decoupaging in the regular way.

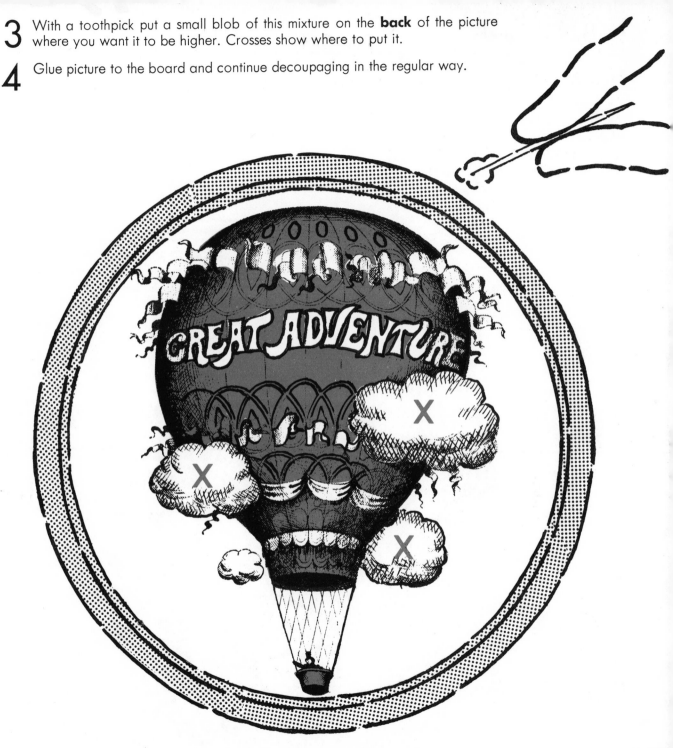

Paper Tole

For this three-dimensional decoupage you need two copies of the same picture and a tube of silica seal. This is sold in craft shops and in hardware stores as bathroom sealer.

You need:
2 copies of the same picture
Silica seal
Acrylic spray
Basic decoupage materials (see chapter 2)

1 Seal the wooden board.

2 Glue on one of the pictures.

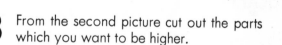

3 From the second picture cut out the parts which you want to be higher.

4 Put big blobs of silica seal on the back of these parts and then put them on the first picture.

5 Spray the decoupage with the acrylic spray.

Framing 3-D Pictures

Stationery boxes with clear plastic lids are perfect for framing knobby and paper tole decoupages. Make your decoupage on the inside of the box. When it is finished, tape the transparent lid back on the box.

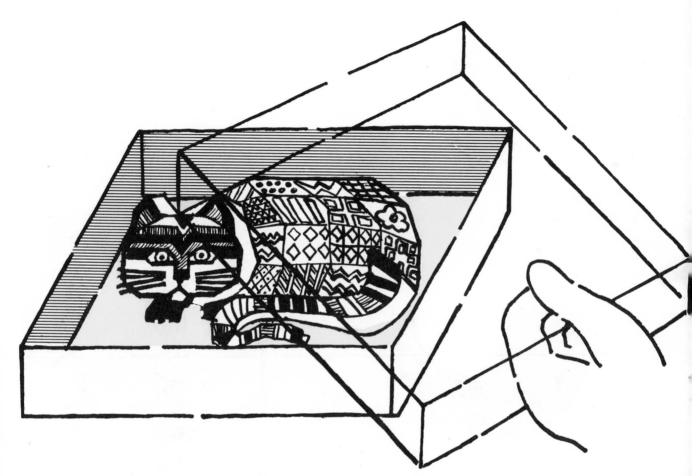

Foil Craft

Aluminum foil and string can turn empty cans and bottles into lovely gifts. The instructions show how to make a savings bank from an empty can. After you have made it you can experiment with other throw-away containers and boxes.

You need:
An empty can with a plastic lid (coffee or nut can)
Felt tip pen
Heavy cotton string (not plastic)
White glue
Q-Tips
Scissors
Acrylic or latex paint, in black or any dark color (there may be
    some leftover paint at your house).
Brush or piece of sponge

1 Draw a design on the can with felt tip pen. If the can has ridges, draw the design in between. Curves and loops are best. You can trace this loop (called paisley) and use it as a pattern. If you do not like the first design you draw, you can redraw with another color felt tip pen, until you like it.

2 Cover one of the felt pen lines with glue. Cut a piece of string and press it into the glue. Cut off extra ends of string. Keep on gluing pieces of string on all the lines until the design is done.

3 Let it dry for about half an hour. Then test to see whether the string is stuck down properly. If there are any loose spots, slide some glue behind with a Q-Tip.

4 Tear off a piece of aluminum foil bigger than you need to cover the whole can. Crumple it up and then smooth it out on a table. Make it flat, but do not try to smooth out all the wrinkles, as they are part of the design.

5 Spread glue over the can. Wrap the foil around the can as evenly as possible.

6 Press the foil down tightly all over. Then use a Q-Tip to push foil even tighter against the string, very gently, so the foil does not tear.

7 At the top, bend the foil to the inside of the can. Also smooth some foil over the bottom of the can. Cut off extra foil.

8 Wipe or brush on paint. Then wipe it off again. This will leave more paint against the ridges next to the string and make the design stand out. Let it dry.

9 Cut a slot in the plastic lid for dropping in coins.

PAINT

Self-stick Decoupage

You have probably found out by now that in decoupage you cover cut-outs and other things with a finish to make them last. Here is another way that is really fun and easy: The finishing coat is ready-made for you and you buy it by the yard. It is transparent plastic film. You may know it as self-stick, Con-Tact, Marvalon or by some other name. It is a wonderful way to make greeting cards and pictures quickly. The instructions show you how to make a greeting card.

You need:

¼ yard transparent self-stick plastic
A piece of paper 7" by 6" (18 cm by 16 cm)
Pressed flowers or flowers cut from stationery or magazines
Scissors
Ruler
White glue
Pencil
Envelopes, commercial size 6¼" by 3¾" (17 cm by 9 cm)

1 Fold paper in half. Size is now 3½" by 6" (9 cm by 16 cm).

2 Place flowers on the outside in a pleasing design.

3 Cut a piece of self-stick 4" by 6½" (10 cm by 17 cm).

4 Cover paper and decoration with the self-stick. Cut the self-stick even with the edge of the greeting card.

Instead of flowers you can use leaves, bits of fabric, feathers, cut-outs, wallpaper samples or souvenirs from a trip. You can do self-stick decoupage on plaques, boxes, frames and other objects.

7

Decoupage Tricks

This chapter shows how to make trick pictures, how to make wood look old, how to line boxes and other ideas to try.

"Fool-the-Eye"

Look at this picture of many cubes for a long time. Are they standing on the floor or are they hanging from the ceiling? Sometimes it seems one way and then it seems the other way. This is called an optical illusion, or a "fool-the-eye" picture. You can make this design by following the instructions, but you have to be exact or the trick will not work.

You need:

A wooden board
Paper in three different colors
A small piece of tracing paper
Pencil and scissors
Sobo or other glue
Basic decoupage materials (see chapter 2)

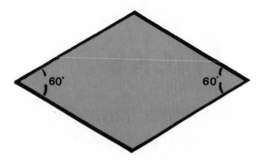

1 Trace this diamond on the tracing paper. Then cut it out.

2 Use this pattern to cut eight diamonds from each piece of colored paper.

3 Sand and seal the board.

4 Arrange the diamonds in the exact pattern shown. Then glue them down carefully.

5 Glaze the picture with Podge or varnish.

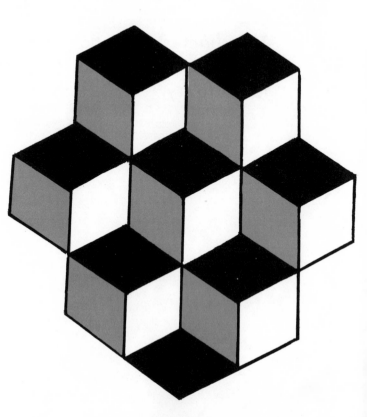

Making Wood Look Old

Many people like to make things look very old, as though they were made many years ago, and perhaps belonged to grandparents. You can do this by wiping on paint or varnish and wiping it off again a little later. This is called "antiquing" (sounds like anteeking). Some special antiquing finishes are for sale in paint, hardware and craft stores. If you decide to use these materials, follow the instructions on the container.

You need:
Any decoupaged object
Walnut stain
Brush or small piece of sponge.

1   Twenty-four hours after your decoupage is finished and completely dry, brush or wipe on the walnut stain.

2   Let it dry for ten minutes. It will be tacky. Wipe object with another piece of sponge, taking off some of the stain, but leaving some streaks. Let dry.

Lining Boxes

If you have made a beautiful box you can make it even better by lining the inside with giftwrap paper. Choose the color of the lining to go well with the outside of the box.

You need:

A decoupaged box
Giftwrap paper to match
Plain paper to make a pattern
Pencil and scissors
White glue

1 First make a pattern from the plain paper. Cut five pieces of paper slightly larger than the sides and the bottom of the box.

2 Press a piece of paper against one inside wall of the box. With your nail or the point of the scissors, scratch around the four edges. Take the paper out of the box and cut on the scratched lines. Paper is now the exact pattern size.

3 Repeat this on the other three inside walls and the bottom of the box. Test all pattern pieces inside box to make sure the sizes are right.

4 Put the pattern pieces on top of the giftwrap and cut out the same sizes.

5 Glue giftwrap inside the box with white glue. Press down firmly all over.

6 Line the lid of the box in the same way.

Glass Decorating

Glasses, jars or bottles can be decoupaged with cut-outs. First wash the glass thoroughly and then clean it again with window cleaner. When the glass is clean and dry, coat it with Podge or white glue and continue with the decoupaging steps shown in chapter 1. (Do not sand.) Decoupaged glass can be used as vases, to hold pencils or cooking tools. Several glasses of the same size look nice in a row.

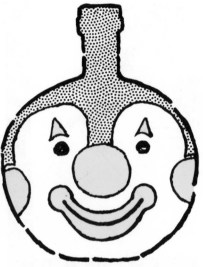

Cut-outs are decoupaged on the outside of a bottle. The round shape of the bottle makes an easy outline for the face.

Cut-outs can be glued to the inside of the glass. Use a glass or jar with a wide mouth. Small cut-outs are easier to use.

These glasses are decorated with transfers.

Framing

Pictures look better in a frame. You can make a frame by gluing a paper border around your design and decoupaging it right along with your picture.

Trimmings

You can use glitter, sequins, paper lace and ready-made borders in your decoupages. Look for them in stationery and craft stores, or cut them out of magazine advertisements. Pieces of paper doilies look good in corners.

8

More Information

This chapter begins with the history of decoupage and is followed by a list of books which tell you more about the craft of decoupage. Next are definitions of the terms used, information about supplies and where to find them in stores, by collecting them or writing away.

The History of Decoupage

The art of decoupage originated in Italy about three hundred years ago. At that time furniture painted with pictures was very popular, but there were not enough artists to supply the demand. For a while, master artists decided just to outline pictures and let assistants fill them in, but even this process was too slow. They decided to print many copies of their designs on paper, paste them on furniture and let the assistants hand color them. They found they could make the finished product look like a regular painting by blending the print with many coats of varnish into a smooth surface. This was the beginning of decoupage. Although it required much time and elbow grease, it was a cheap way of brightening a chest or chair, and for this reason it became known as "the poor man's art," *l'arte del povere,* in Italian.

In later years it became fashionable to import painted furniture from the Orient. Decoupage was again used to imitate this desirable style of furniture. Some pieces of furniture were decorated in the tricky way called *trompe l'oeil,* a French word meaning "fool-the-eye." You might call it old-fashioned op art. A typical trompe l'oeil piece of furniture was a desk with a bookcase on top. All sorts of things stood on the desk: an inkwell, a quill pen, parchment paper and a few coins. The doors of the bookcase were open, showing handsome leatherbound books inside. From a distance you might admire the desk and want to look at one of the books. However, when you reached for it, you would discover that the whole thing was a painted picture. Only by touching it would you realize it was fake, done with perspective painting.

Although decoupage started as an imitation of painting, it developed into a definite art form. Skill is required to combine the parts of the print into a well-balanced composition. Experimenting with various finishes produces better-looking and longer-lasting objects.

In the eighteenth century, decoupage developed into a hobby which became wildly popular when the French Queen Marie Antoinette tried her hand at it. Pictures were painted by famous artists and reproduced in thousands of printed copies for decoupaging by the queen's ladies-in-waiting and other hobbyists. They cut up the prints and colored them, like modern painting-by-number kits. When the object was varnished it looked as though it was beautifully hand-painted. This method was used not only to decorate furniture but boxes, screens, fans and wall decorations.

The decoupaging fad spread all over Europe and then to the United States, but like any fad, it did not last forever and during the 1800's other crafts became popular. Furniture was carved instead of painted. Valentines and pictures were now embossed or pinpricked, rather than decoupaged. Decoupage was not practiced again until about thirty years ago. One reason for the revival is the invention of new plastic glues and varnishes, which make it possible to decoupage much faster than in olden days, although experts still spend many weeks on making one piece. Designs can be nostalgic or in the latest fashion, and there is no limit to the ways in which you can combine cut paper, paint, glue and varnish.

Helpful Hints and Information

Acrylic spray: This is used as a sealer. or a glaze. It is sometimes called craft spray, clear acrylic sealer or by a brand name, such as Krylon. Three spray coats equal one brush coat.

Air bubbles: They form under the paper when it is glued down. They have to be pressed out, or they may show up again weeks later.

Basic decoupage materials: 1. An object to be decoupaged
2. A decoration (print or cut-out)
3. Podge (or sealer, glue and varnish) with brush or piece of sponge
4. Sandpaper, if you are using a wooden object
5. Spoon or roller
6. Scissors

Board: Use a piece of wood you find at home or a wooden board especially made for. decoupage, also called a plaque.

Brayer: See roller.

Canvas board: Sold in art stores. Cover them with gesso before decoupaging.

Craft spray: See acrylic spray.

Edges of prints and cut-outs: Always press edges down firmly.

Gesso: A thick creamy liquid which levels uneven surfaces. Useful for smoothing rough wood, canvas board or rocks.

Glazes: All sorts of products can be used for glazes. The most important are Podge, white glue, acrylic spray and many kinds of varnishes.

Glues: White glues made from a plastic called polyvinyl acetate (PVA) are best. Some are thicker or thinner or have chemicals added for a special use; you really can use any of them. Sobo is best; Elmer's Glue-All needs more rolling and longer drying. Acrylic Medium (Hyplar and other brands) can also be used.

Medium: Use it as a glue or varnish.

Modeling paste: For building up knobs and bumps in 3-D decoupage.

Paint: Paints are used to color the background before pasting on prints and cut-outs, or to paint a complete picture. Acrylic, latex and oil paints can be used on wood, cardboard, papier-mâché, glass, ceramics or metal. Acrylic paints are easier to use than oil, as they can easily be washed off with water when they are still wet. But they dry hard very quickly, and cannot then be washed off at all. If you cover the whole background with acrylic paint, you do not need a sealer first. For painting pale backgrounds, thin acrylic paint with water or acrylic medium. Any acrylic paint brand is suitable; some well-known ones are: Hyplar, Liquitex, Shiva and Patricia Nimocks.

Plaque: A wooden board made especially for decoupage, usually with shaped edges.

Podge: A glue product which can be used for sealing, gluing and glazing. Mod-Podge, Fun Podge and Twinkle Podge are brand names. It is a good idea to cover a podged decoupage with a coat of polyurethane, but not essential. Instead of Podge you can use white glue for sealing or gluing, and varnish for glazing.

Polyurethane: A plastic varnish which can be brushed, wiped or sprayed. It makes a very hard finish, good for trays or coasters.

Roller: Every print or cut-out has to be rolled when it is glued down or air bubbles may appear later. You can use the back of a spoon, a 4″ decoupage brayer, or a wallpaper roller.

Sanding: Wood has to be smoothed down with sandpaper. For really professional-looking decoupages you have to sand every coat of glaze before you put on another coat. Sand with the grain of the wood, that is in the direction of the long lines. Sandpaper is cheapest in hardware stores, but is also sold in decoupage supply shops. You need a fine-grade number 000 or "garnet." Wrap it around a wooden block.

Sealing: Wood is sealed with Podge or acrylic spray to make it smoother. Paper prints are easier to cut when they have first been sealed with acrylic spray or sealer and the ink colors do not run.

Spray finishing: See acrylic spray.

Stain: Stains can be used to darken wood. If you decide to use them, follow the directions on the can and remember to stain **before** sealing.

Stenciling: Stencils can be used for decoupage designs.

Transfer: You can buy transfer liquids where decoupage supplies are sold. Some brands are: decal-it, Trans-A-Print or Hypage.

Wax: A coat of wax over the completed decoupage gives a nice finish. Use household waxes.

White glue: See glues.

Wipers: Small pieces of sponge or felt, about 1″ square, can be used to wipe on finishes. Throw them away after use. They are used instead of brushes, which have to be washed and cleaned.

Varnishes: Any transparent coating is a varnish. Podge, white glue or varnishes from the paint store can be used. Deft is a good brand.

Where to Find Materials

You can find most things you need at the supermarket, variety store or hardware store, but an arts and crafts store will have the best selection and the salesperson can help you with advice about the craft. You can write away for supplies to these companies:

For almost anything you need: glues, trimmings, prints, etc.

Adventures in Crafts, Inc.
218 East 81st Street
New York, New York 10028

American Handicrafts Company
Fort Worth, Texas 76101

Connoisseur Studios, Inc.
Box 7187
Louisville, Kentucky 40207

Harrower House of Decoupage
37 Carpenter Street
Box 502
Milford, New Jersey 08848

Hazel Pearson Handicrafts
41287 Temple City Boulevard
Rosemead, California 91770

For new and old-fashioned prints and trimmings:

Brandon Memorabilia, Inc.
1 West 30th Street
New York, New York 10001

But the most fun is looking for decorations anywhere. Sometimes you may be walking along the street and find a leaf, or your parents may bring home a shopping bag printed with a bright picture; or you may decide to decoupage a poem. Keep your eyes open for bits and pieces of unusual shape. Keep all these things in a box; you may not use them right away, but later on they may be just what you need.

More Reading

If you want to know more about decoupage, here are the names of some adult books:

Decoupage, by Leslie Linsley; Doubleday & Company, Inc., Garden City, N.Y., 1972

Contemporary Decoupage, by Thelma Newman; Crown Publishers, Inc., New York, 1972

The Craft of Decoupage, by Patricia E. Nimocks; Charles Scribner's Sons, New York, 1972.

About the Author

FLORENCE TEMKO is a well-known author in the craft field, whose previous books include *Paper Cutting*, *Felt Craft* and *Self-Stick Craft* in this series, as well as the authoritative *Paper: Folded, Cut, Sculpted*. She thinks crafts are wonderful and shows people just what they want to make. She also spreads her enthusiasm through lectures, films, television appearances and her newspaper column *Things to Make*. She studied at the London School of Economics and the New School for Social Research in New York and has taught at schools, colleges, museums (including the Metropolitan Museum of Art in New York), libraries and is a consultant to industry. She now lives in Lenox, Massachusetts.

About the Artist

LINDA WINCHESTER is a free-lance artist who specializes in graphics and three-dimensional design. She is a graduate of the Layton School of Art in Milwaukee, has worked at *New York* magazine, Hallmark Cards and Norcross and collaborated with Florence Temko on a previous book: *Self-Stick Craft*. Born in the Midwest, she now lives in the Berkshire Hills of Massachusetts.

DATE DUE

APR 23 '80			
MAY 8 '80			
SEP 23 '80			
MAY 6 '81			
MAR 15 '82			
NOV 15 '83			
MAR 16 '84			
APR 29			
APR. 7			
MAY 18			
NOV 9			
GAYLORD			PRINTED IN U.S.A.